A TITANIC TIME CAPSULE

ARTIFACTS OF THE SUNKEN SHIP

by Jessica Freeburg

Consultant:
Richard Bell, PhD
Associate Professor of History
University of Maryland, College Park

CAPSTONE PRESS
a capstone imprint

Capstone Captivate is published by Capstone Press, an imprint of Capstone.
1710 Roe Crest Drive
North Mankato, Minnesota 56003
www.capstonepub.com

Library of Congress Cataloging-in-Publication Data is available
on the Library of Congress website.
ISBN: 978-1-5435-9233-7 (library binding)
ISBN: 978-1-4966-6631-4 (paperback)
ISBN: 978-1-5435-9240-5 (eBook pdf)

Summary: Consider opening a chamber to discover an antique violin, a yellowed
menu, and a tattered coat. Together these artifacts can be used to tell of the
splendor of the luxury ship *Titanic* and its tragic sinking in 1912. Open this
imaginary time capsule and explore one of history's most fascinating events.

Image Credits
Alamy: Shawshots, 14, WENN Rights Ltd., 21, Wild Places Photography/
Chris Howes, 36; AP: The Register-Guard/Chris Pietsch, 30; Dreamstime:
Jeffreymetcalf31, 25; Getty Images: The LIFE Images Collection/Cynthia
Johnson, 41; Library of Congress: 8, 16, 31, 39; Mary Evans Picture Library:
Illustrated London News Ltd., 9, Onslow Auctions Limited, 12; Newscom: akg-
images, 18, 37, Album/Fine Art Images, 7, El Tiempo de Colombia/GDA, 40,
Everett Collection, 15, Mirrorpix/Daily Mirror, 13, Richard B. Levine, 42, Sipa
Press/Anthony Behar, cover (top right), 17, 26, Splash News, 22, Splash News/
Solent News, cover (left), United Archives/Carl Simon Archive, cover (middle), 5,
28; North Wind Picture Archives: 34; Shutterstock: ale-kup (background), cover
and throughout, chrisdorney, 11, Everett Historical, 32, 33, 38, Jane Rix, 43

Editorial Credits
Editor: Julie Gassman; Designers: Lori Bye and Bobbie Nuytten;
Media Researcher: Svetlana Zhurkin; Production Specialist: Tori Abraham

Table of Contents

Words in **bold** are in the glossary.

CHAPTER 1
INTRODUCTION

When something important happens, we want to remember it. One of the ways we can do so is to save special things from that event. Artifacts such as letters, clothing, and artwork can be evidence that helps to prove what happened, shows how people reacted, and reminds us what was important about that moment in time. This collection of items could even be kept in a time capsule—a container of artifacts hidden away for discovery in the future.

What if there were a special time capsule for each important moment in history? What if you found one of these time capsules? What might be in it?

The *Titanic* sank in the North Atlantic Ocean on April 15, 1912. The ship was more than 882 feet (269 meters) long and weighed 46,000 tons (41,730 metric tons). The passenger **liner** broke apart before dropping to the ocean floor. It remained hidden for more than 70 years. In many ways, it became the ultimate time capsule. Many of the personal belongings of its passengers lie in and around the broken ship.

CHAPTER 2
SETTING SAIL ABOARD THE *TITANIC*

From the Time Capsule:
POSTER FOR THE *TITANIC*

Imagine standing in front of a time capsule the size of a large shed. You wonder what could be in it. After climbing a ladder, you look inside.

You reach for a paper rolled up like a scroll. As you unroll it, you see a poster. It says, "The World's Largest Liner." The picture shows a huge ship beside a smaller boat.

You run your finger over the letters across the top. T-I-T-A-N-I-C. You imagine how excited people were when they looked at this poster more than one hundred years ago.

The White Star Line's newest ship was like a floating castle. It was about 17 stories high. The **hull** was four city blocks long. At the time, it was the largest ship ever built.

Fact

The White Star Line created three sister ships—the *Titanic*, the *Olympic*, and the *Britannic*. Both the *Titanic* and the *Britannic* sank.

Located in first class, the Veranda café featured wicker cane furniture and large windows that looked out to the ocean.

There were nine decks with a total of 416 first-class cabins, 162 second-class cabins, and 262 third-class cabins. It had 16 **watertight compartments** designed to be sealed shut if the ship was damaged. Many thought the *Titanic* was unsinkable.

The wealthiest passengers traveled in first class. They could enjoy a saltwater pool, **Turkish baths**, and 10-course meals. The *Titanic* was the first ship to have a gym—with the latest exercise equipment and **squash** courts.

Second-class cabin rooms were as comfortable as first-class rooms on other ships. Even third-class rooms were nicer than those on other liners. The *Titanic* was designed for all its passengers to enjoy.

The gym gave passengers the opportunity to exercise during their journey.

FLYER TO ADVERTISE TICKETS

You might look into the time capsule and see a yellowed booklet. Picking it up, you read, "The World's Largest & Finest Steamers." This **brochure** advertised tickets for the White Star Line's luxury ships.

Traveling on ships was very common at the time. But being one of the first to sail on the *Titanic* would have felt special. It was said to be the finest ship on the ocean. People were excited to see it.

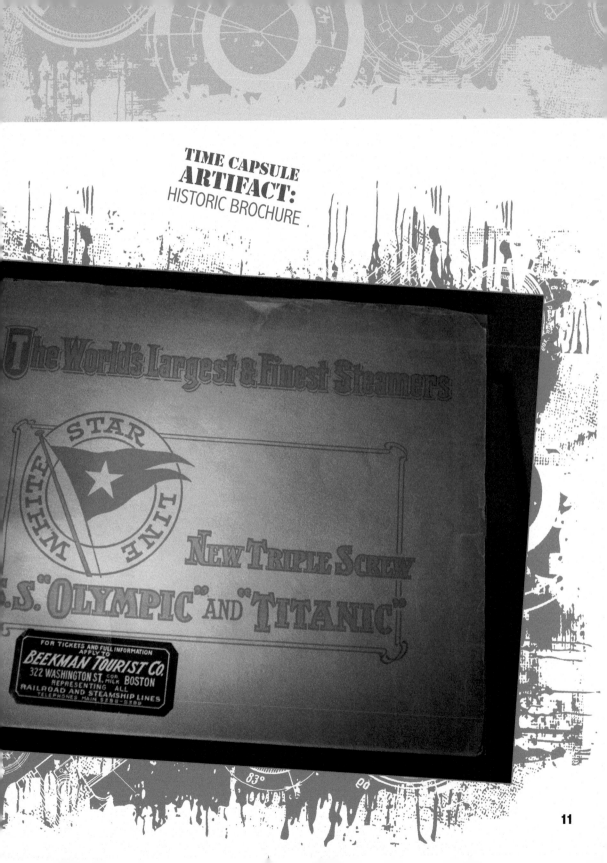

The World's Largest & Finest Steamers

WHITE STAR LINE

NEW TRIPLE SCREW

S.S. "OLYMPIC" AND "TITANIC"

FOR TICKETS AND FULL INFORMATION
APPLY TO
BEEKMAN TOURIST CO.
322 WASHINGTON ST. COR. MILK BOSTON
REPRESENTING ALL
RAILROAD AND STEAMSHIP LINES
TELEPHONES MAIN 5288-5289

Captain Edward J. Smith's nickname was "the Millionaire's Captain" because he was popular with wealthy passengers.

Passengers boarded the *Titanic* in Southampton, England, on April 10, 1912. Their destination was New York City. There were 324 passengers in first class, 284 in second class, and 709 in third. Because there were so many passengers in third class, they got on first. Passengers in second class boarded next. **Stewards** greeted them and showed them to their cabins. Captain Edward J. Smith personally welcomed passengers with first-class tickets while stewards gathered their luggage and delivered it to their rooms.

Foreshadow of Dangers Ahead

When the *Titanic* left the docks, it created large waves. This caused a smaller ship to break away from its **mooring**. The two boats almost crashed. Passenger Charlotte Collyer recalled, "It did not frighten anyone, as it only seemed to prove how powerful the *Titanic* was." No one dreamed it foreshadowed a greater disaster to come.

CHAPTER 3

DISASTER AT SEA

From the Time Capsule:
MENU FROM THE SHIP

Perhaps you look back into the time capsule. Maybe there is a half-sheet of paper, yellowed by time. It is a third-class menu for April 14, 1912. These are some of the last meals eaten by the passengers who went down with the ship. You imagine the men, women, and children in third class enjoying ham and eggs as they started the fourth day of their trip.

TIME CAPSULE
ARTIFACT:
SHIP'S MENU

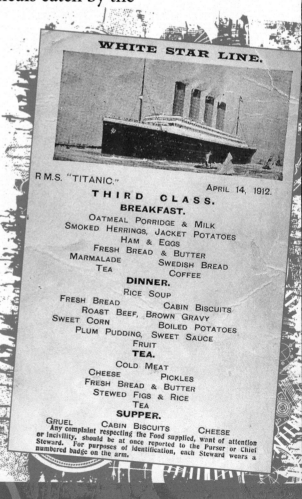

WHITE STAR LINE.

R.M.S. "TITANIC."   APRIL 14, 1912.

THIRD CLASS.

BREAKFAST.

OATMEAL PORRIDGE & MILK
SMOKED HERRINGS, JACKET POTATOES
HAM & EGGS
FRESH BREAD & BUTTER
MARMALADE   SWEDISH BREAD
TEA   COFFEE

DINNER.

RICE SOUP
FRESH BREAD   CABIN BISCUITS
ROAST BEEF, BROWN GRAVY
SWEET CORN   BOILED POTATOES
PLUM PUDDING, SWEET SAUCE
FRUIT

TEA.

COLD MEAT
CHEESE   PICKLES
FRESH BREAD & BUTTER
STEWED FIGS & RICE
TEA

SUPPER.

GRUEL   CABIN BISCUITS   CHEESE
Any complaint respecting the Food supplied, want of attention or incivility, should be at once reported to the Purser or Chief Steward. For purposes of identification, each Steward wears a numbered badge on the arm.

Passengers of all ages enjoyed the boat decks, the only open areas on the ship.

April 14, 1912, began well. Passengers strolled along the decks. Some enjoyed the libraries and gym. They shared meals with friends. Some passengers walked their dogs. Children explored and played games together.

Lady Duff-Gordon

Lady Duff-Gordon, a British survivor who traveled in first class, remembered a beautiful vase of fresh daffodils at her table during dinner that night. While she enjoyed her meal, passengers around her visited. They placed bets on when the *Titanic* would arrive in the United States. They had no way of knowing the ship would never reach the shore. For more than two thirds of them, this would be their final meal.

The sun shone brightly during the first three days. On the fourth day, the skies were gray. But the sea remained perfectly calm. As evening set in, many people went to their rooms to go to sleep. Others visited a little longer in the lounge. They were unaware of the danger ahead of them.

From the Time Capsule:
BINOCULARS

TIME CAPSULE
ARTIFACT:
BINOCULARS

If you reached into the time capsule again, you might touch something with rounded edges. The metal surface would feel cool against your skin. You might lift it out to look at it more closely.

You would be holding a pair of binoculars found in the wreckage of the *Titanic*. These binoculars could have prevented the tragedy that put the *Titanic* on the ocean floor. But the lookouts could not get to them.

The ship began to receive wireless messages from other boats at 9:00 a.m. These messages warned them of ice sheets and icebergs spotted in the area. Lookouts were told to watch for icebergs. The ship continued on at full speed.

Frederick Fleet and Reginald Lee were lookouts that night. The men did not have binoculars, which were stored in a locked box. The officer who had the key was assigned to a different ship before the *Titanic* set sail. When he left, he forgot to give the key to the officer who replaced him. Fleet later said that if he had binoculars, they would have likely seen the iceberg in time to avoid hitting it.

Fleet finally spotted the iceberg and rang the lookout bell three times. Then he called the **bridge**. But it was too late. The ship could not turn fast enough. At 11:40 p.m., the *Titanic* sideswiped the iceberg.

Survivors estimated that the iceberg towered between 50 to 100 feet (15 to 30 meters) above water.

Many passengers who weren't sleeping yet felt the ship vibrate. Some were woken up by the impact. Most were not concerned by the slight disturbance. As the ship came to a stop, few suspected anything was seriously wrong. But five of the watertight compartments were damaged. Water was quickly filling them. If fewer compartments had been damaged, sealing them off from the rest of the ship could have prevented the ship from sinking. But five damaged compartments taking in water from the ocean would prove to be more than the ship could bear. Before long, the **bow** began to dip lower into the ocean as the water steadily rose inside.

Wires of Warning

Senior wireless operator Jack Phillips received a final warning about ice in the area about 40 minutes before the *Titanic* hit the iceberg. Because the wireless transmitter had broken down the day before, Phillips was trying to catch up on sending out messages for passengers. He set the warning aside and returned to his work. The warning never made it to Captain Smith.

TIME CAPSULE
ARTIFACT:
LIFE JACKET

Beneath the papers and binoculars, you might find a tan life jacket from the *Titanic*. You let the straps slide through your fingers. These thin pieces of fabric once held the life jacket securely on Laura Mabel Francatelli, a passenger in first class.

Laura Mabel Francatelli (third from right, standing) with the other survivors from her lifeboat

Francatelli was Lady Duff-Gordon's secretary. After the crash, she noticed water seeping into her bedroom. She told Duff-Gordon. A crew member came by and told them to put on life jackets. He said not to worry. The life jackets were simply a precaution. When they reached the deck, it seemed clear to Francatelli that the ship was sinking. The water level had already risen closer to the deck.

The bow dipped deeper into the water. Still, many passengers did not believe the *Titanic* would sink. Some were afraid to get into the lifeboats. They thought they would be safer staying on the large ship than floating in the ocean in a tiny boat.

Fact

The *Titanic* had 20 lifeboats. They could hold 1,178 of the approximately 2,220 people on board. But many lifeboats were launched only half full.

If you set down the life jacket and look back into the capsule, a violin with just two strings might catch your eye. This violin belonged to Wallace Hartley. He was the leader of the *Titanic*'s band. You pick it up. It is in surprisingly good condition. The violin is more than 100 years old. It spent many days in the salty ocean water.

Many described the atmosphere on the *Titanic* during those final hours as calm and orderly. The captain ordered that women and children should be the first to board lifeboats. Some women argued to stay with their husbands. But most were persuaded to get into the lifeboats. The men remained calm. Many assured their wives and children they would see them soon.

All the while, the band, directed by Wallace Hartley, played on the deck. They played until the deck slanted too much for them to continue. All eight musicians went down with the ship. Only three of their bodies were recovered, including Hartley's. Strapped to Hartley's back was his music case. Inside was the violin he played as the *Titanic* was sinking.

TIME CAPSULE
ARTIFACT:
VIOLIN

From the Time Capsule:
MAN'S VEST AND POCKET WATCH

TIME CAPSULE
ARTIFACT:
VEST AND WATCH

What else might you discover in your time capsule? Looking around, you might notice a man's vest and pocket watch. They belonged to a passenger in third class. The fabric looks worn. But it is hard to believe this vest was on the bottom of the ocean for more than 70 years. You wonder if the man who owned these things was one of the few men from the third-class section of the ship to survive.

Many passengers in third class were **immigrants**. Laws required them to be kept separated from the other passengers. This ensured they could be processed when they arrived in the United States. Because of this, many of the passages to the upper decks remained locked.

Survivor Daniel Buckley recalled that as he and other men in the third-class section tried to get to the first-class deck, a man pushed them back and locked a gate. The passengers in third class broke the lock and forced their way through.

As it became clearer that the ship was sinking, panic began to set in among the passengers.

When Buckley arrived on the deck, there were no women or children in the area. He jumped into a boat with a group of men. But two officers arrived with female passengers and told the men to get out.

As the women got in, Buckley began to cry. He feared that if he got out of the lifeboat, he would die. One woman told Buckley to stay. She put her shawl over him, hiding him. The officers finished loading the boat and lowered it into the water.

Fact

The *Titanic* hit the iceberg at 11:40 p.m. It disappeared under the water at 2:20 a.m. It took the ship just 2 hours and 40 minutes to sink.

CHAPTER 4

SURVIVING THE SINKING

From the Time Capsule:
SURVIVOR'S COAT

If you reached into the time capsule once again, you might feel the thick, coarse wool of a coat. It was worn by one of the survivors the night the *Titanic* sank. You hold it to your chest and breathe in the musty odor of time. You imagine the survivor shivering beneath the fabric, both from the cold air and from the shock of what was happening.

TIME CAPSULE
ARTIFACT:
WOOL COAT

Many of the passengers had already gone to bed when the *Titanic* hit the iceberg. Some quickly dressed before going to the deck. Many others simply put coats over their pajamas. The temperature had dropped near freezing. Women and children huddled together in lifeboats to stay warm.

Wireless officer Harold Bride was washed off the ship as it went underwater. In the chaos of the final moments, the last lifeboat tipped over. Bride managed to climb on top of it. He and 15 other men clung to the top of the overturned boat. They prayed it would not sink beneath them.

Harold Bride suffered injuries to his feet, including severe frostbite.

Hundreds of passengers jumped into the freezing ocean as the *Titanic* plunged beneath the surface. The water was 28 degrees Fahrenheit (minus 2.2 degrees Celsius). **Hypothermia** occurs in water temperatures between 30 and 40°F (–1.1 and 4.4°C). It is typically fatal within 30 to 90 minutes. The *Carpathia* arrived nearly two hours after the *Titanic* went under. By then, most of the victims in the water had died.

From the Time Capsule:
TITANIC LIFEBOAT

TIME CAPSULE
ARTIFACT:
LIFEBOAT

Setting the coat down, you might peer over the side of the time capsule. You pull yourself up and swing your legs over the edge. You drop into the capsule and land in a wooden boat. You are standing inside one of *Titanic*'s lifeboats.

The lifeboats rowed away, some only half full. Those inside looked back at the ship. The lower decks began to sink beneath the surface. Hundreds of the people still on the *Titanic* lined the upper decks. As the water rose, most people hurried upward. They wanted to stay on the ship as long as possible. Some feared they would drown if they were sucked deep under the water with the ship when it went down.

The passengers left floating in the freezing water screamed for help. Their cries joined the roar of the *Titanic* busting apart and thundering downward.

Some passengers were able to climb atop an overturned boat after surviving the sinking.

Many of the survivors in the lifeboats wanted to paddle toward the victims in the ocean. But others feared people desperate to get into the boats might overturn them. When the screams stopped, people in at least one lifeboat rowed back to see if they could save anyone. They were too late.

Fact

Survivor Violet Jessop, a stewardess on the *Titanic*, was on all three of the White Star Line's luxury sister ships when they were involved in disasters. She was on the *Olympic* when it collided with a British warship in 1911. She was also a survivor on the *Britannic*, the *Titanic*'s sister ship, when it sank in 1916 due to an unexplained explosion.

NEWSPAPER ARTICLE REPORTING TRAGEDY

Looking over the edge of the lifeboat into the time capsule, you see a yellowed newspaper page dated April 21, 1912. The headline: "1,463 LIVES LOST. THE WORLD'S GREATEST LINER COLLIDES WITH ICEBERG" tops the story in black letters. You scan the subtitle: "AWFUL SCENES DESCRIBED BY SURVIVORS." You read about how the survivors were rescued. You learn about the efforts made to recover the bodies of those who lost their lives.

TIME CAPSULE ARTIFACT:
HISTORIC NEWSPAPER

The *Carpathia* arrived at the scene at 4:00 a.m., about three and a half hours after receiving the call for help.

The cries for help faded into silence. Survivors in lifeboats drifted under a starlit sky. They would wait for hours. They prayed someone would respond to the *Titanic*'s distress messages. The *Carpathia* answered the call. It sailed hundreds of miles to reach them.

Fact

Nine-year-old passenger Frankie Goldsmith huddled with his mother in a lifeboat as his father went down with the ship. Later, they lived in Detroit near the baseball stadium. The sound of fans screaming for a home run haunted him. They sounded too much like the cries of those who went into the water with the *Titanic*.

As they sailed on the *Carpathia*, most of the survivors suffered from shock and were grieving for their losses.

Survivors were brought on board the *Carpathia* one by one. Women and children hoped the husbands and fathers they'd left behind on the *Titanic* would be pulled into the safety of the *Carpathia*. But very few would be reunited with the men they loved.

The *Carpathia* traveled to New York City. It carried hundreds of widows and fatherless children. An estimated 10,000 people were at the harbor when the ship arrived on April 18, 1912. The crowd included journalists, photographers, and friends and relatives of the survivors.

Several other ships were sent to retrieve the bodies of those who died. They lacked the room and resources to transport them all to land. So, most of the bodies were buried at sea.

One survivor said the crowd that waited for the *Carpathia*'s arrival stood in "an intense silence, a silence of death."

CHAPTER 5

REMEMBERING THE *TITANIC*

From the Time Capsule:
DEEP-SEA SUB *ALVIN*

As you look up from the newspaper article, you might see a white submarine nearby. Looking up, you see a red box on top. It says "Alvin." *Alvin* was the first **submersible** to carry humans to the bottom of the ocean to visit the *Titanic*. In a way, this small submarine brought life back to the ship.

TIME CAPSULE
ARTIFACT:
ALVIN

The luxury ship nicknamed the "Queen of the Ocean" sat at the bottom of the Atlantic, undisturbed. Scientists and explorers searched for more than 70 years, hoping to find the vessel. Finally, on September 1, 1985, the wreckage was found by deep-sea explorer Robert Ballard.

Robert Ballard

The wreckage is almost 2 miles (3.2 km) beneath the surface of the water. It stretches for nearly a mile across the ocean floor. *Alvin* made its first trip to the site in 1986. At that depth, the water is pitch black. But with modern equipment, scientists photographed the wreckage and recovered some items from the debris.

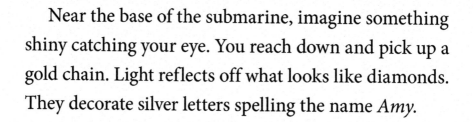

**TIME CAPSULE
ARTIFACT:**
BRACELET

Near the base of the submarine, imagine something shiny catching your eye. You reach down and pick up a gold chain. Light reflects off what looks like diamonds. They decorate silver letters spelling the name *Amy*.

You can almost see the bracelet on the wrist of a young woman wearing a fashionable dress. You hope she was among those who survived. More than seven decades after the bracelet slipped into the ocean, it was brought to the surface. Whom the bracelet belonged to remains a mystery.

Passengers on the *Titanic* were from many different countries. Cities around the world have memorials to the *Titanic*, including New York and Southampton, England. The tragedy led to improved safety precautions on ocean liners. Hundreds of artifacts have been recovered from the wreckage. These artifacts help us remember those who died. They let us see what life was like more than a century ago.

A memorial in Southampton, England, honors the ship's engineers, who remained at their posts until the ship sank.

More About the Artifacts

Poster for the *Titanic*

The British shipping company White Star Line commissioned this poster and others to promote travel on its luxury ocean liner the *Titanic*. The poster was probably created in early 1912, and today it is part of a private collection.

Flyer to Advertise Tickets

White Star Line promoted its ships *Olympic* and *Titanic* with marketing materials such as this brochure. This rare artifact is on display at the *Titanic* Belfast Museum in Northern Ireland, which is located in the same area where the *Titanic* was built and launched.

Menu from the *Titanic*

This menu was created by White Star Line for the passengers in third class. Historians presume that the menu was saved by passengers who escaped onto lifeboats as the ship took on water.

Binoculars

These binoculars were found in the **crow's nest** of the *Titanic* when the wreckage was discovered. The binoculars were sold in a lot of 5,000 artifacts in an auction conducted by Guernsey's in New York City in 2012.

Life Jacket

Made out of cork that is covered with canvas, Laura Mabel Francatelli's life jacket is one of 12 remaining from the *Titanic*. After being rescued by the *Carpathia*, Francatelli asked the other 11 passengers on her lifeboat to sign the life jacket. Many of the signatures can still be seen on the preserver, which last sold in a 2007 auction by Christie's in South Kensington, England, for $118,643.

Wallace Hartley's Violin

Misplaced for many years, Wallace Hartley's rosewood violin was believed to be lost at sea. But in 2006, it was discovered in the attic of a home in the United Kingdom. After seven years of scientific testing and historic research, experts confirmed it was indeed Hartley's violin. Originally, the violin was a gift from Hartley's fiancée, Maria Robinson. A special engraving is one of the most important pieces of evidence of its origin. It reads, "For Wallace on the occasion of our engagement from Maria."

Man's Vest and Pocket Watch

This vest and watch were found in a suitcase that was recovered from the wreckage in 2000. Many of the pieces of clothing in the suitcase were stamped "W. Allen," indicating that they belonged to William Henry Allen, a toolmaker from England. Allen traveled in third class and was 35 years old when he drowned. The vest and pocket watch were part of the Guernsey auction in 2012.

Survivor's Coat

This Marion Wright Woolcott wore this wool coat while escaping the sinking ship. Woolcott lived the remainder of her life in Cottage Grove, Oregon. After her death, her son donated the coat to the Cottage Grove Historical Museum, which often loans out the coat to other museums.

Titanic Lifeboat

The *Titanic* had 20 lifeboats on board. After the passengers were rescued, the *Carpathia* had room for only 13 of the boats. The other seven were left behind. Once the *Carpathia* reached New York City, the 13 boats were unloaded, and White Star Line employees removed their nameplates. Without the markings, there was no way to track the boats from that point, but some historians believe they were given new nameplates and used on the sister ship, the *Olympic*.

Newspaper Article Reporting Tragedy

News of the World published this newspaper issue on April 21, 1912, a week after the tragedy. The headline, like most headlines of the day, reported an incorrect death toll of 1,463. (Experts estimate that 1,517 people were killed.) The errors were largely due to conflicting reports being radioed in from other ships.

Deep-Sea Sub *Alvin*

The submersible was commissioned on June 5, 1964, by the U.S. Navy. It was built by the company General Mills in Minneapolis, Minnesota. About every three years, the *Alvin* is overhauled to upgrade pieces as needed. All of its parts have been replaced at least once.

"Amy" Bracelet

Recovered from the wreckage in 1987, the "Amy" bracelet was also part of the 5,000 artifacts sold in the Guernsey auction in 2012. It is made of 15-karat rose gold, silver, and diamonds. At least two people on the *Titanic* were named Amy, with one being a member of the crew. Historians say it could have also belonged to passengers named Amelia or Amanda.

Glossary

bow (BOU)—the front end of a ship

bridge (BRIJ)—the control center of a ship

brochure (broh-SHOOR)—a paper or small book used to promote or advertise something

crow's nest (KROHZ NEST)—a lookout post located high above a ship

hull (HUHL)—the main, lowermost body of a ship

hypothermia (hye-poh-THUR-mee-uh)—a life-threatening condition that occurs when the body temperature dips below the normal range as a result of exposure to extreme cold

immigrant (IM-uh-gruhnt)—a person who leaves one country to live in another

liner (LYE-ner)—a ship operated by a transportation company

mooring (MOR-ing)—cables used to secure a ship to a dock

squash (SKWAHSH)—a game played in a specially designed court where two to four players hit a small, rubber ball with a racket against the walls

steward (STOO-urd)—a person who attends to the needs of passengers on a ship; a female steward is called a stewardess

submersible (suhb-MUR-suh-buhl)—a device or vessel that can be used to explore underwater

Turkish bath (TUR-kihsh BATH)—a relaxing treatment that involves time in a steam room followed by a massage

watertight compartment (WAW-tur-tite kuhm-PART-muhnt)—area within the ship designed to be sealed in case of damage or leaking

Read More

Otfinski, Steven. *Smooth Sea and a Fighting Chance: The Story of the Sinking of the* Titanic. North Mankato, MN: Capstone Press, 2016.

Sabol, Stephanie. *What Was the* Titanic? New York: Penguin Random House, 2018.

Terrell, Brandon. *Stories of* Titanic's *Crew.* Mankato, MN: Child's World, 2016.

Internet Sites

Encyclopedia Titanica
https://www.encyclopedia-Titanica.org

National Geographic Kids
https://www.natgeokids.com/uk/discover/history/general-history/would-you-have-survived-the-Titanic/

Science Kids
http://www.sciencekids.co.nz/sciencefacts/engineering/Titanic.html

Titanic *Facts and History*
http://www.Titanicfactsandhistory.com/Titanic-facts-for-kids/

Index